ATG Studies

The Whole-Heart Journey®

"Understanding the Process: Initiate Level"

Written by

Dr. Debbye Graafsma, bcpc

The Whole Heart Journey™-
Class One – "Understanding the Process"
Initiate Level Workbook
ISBN -- 978-0-9893214-9-5
First edition publish date: October, 2024

To contact us:
Awakened to Grow.com
email: awakenedtogrow@gmail.com

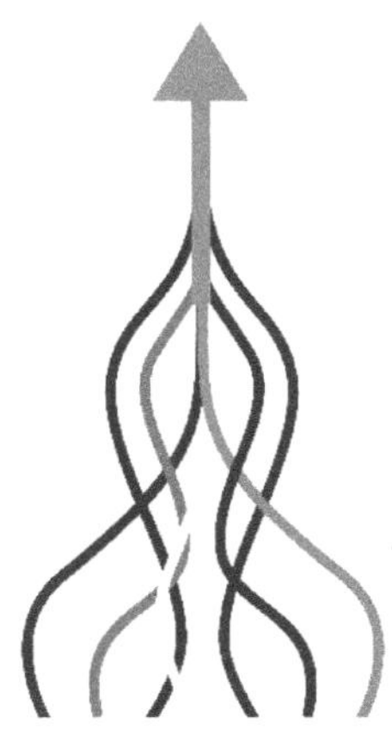

Spirit, Will, Thoughts, Emotions, Appetites, Impulses

The Whole Heart Journey™ –

"Understanding the Process"

Initiate Level Workbook

Individual Journaling Workbook

The Whole Heart Journey ™ -- Understanding the Process

This workbook is designed to accompany recorded video teaching sessions, available online or by ordering from our web address: www.wholeheartjourney.net.

Table of Contents

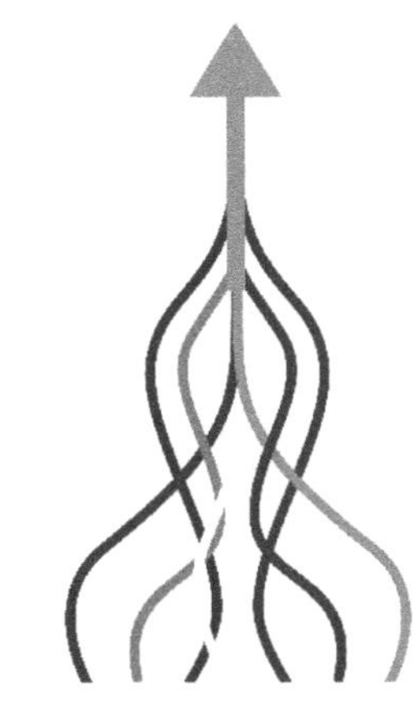

Spirit, Will, Thoughts, Emotions, Appetites, Impulses

The Whole Heart Journey™ –

"Understanding the Process"

Initiate Level Workbook

Introductory Session

(Please utilize the Introduction Video as you work through the pages for this Session.)

(Please watch the beginning of the Introduction Session Video here.)

What is The Whole Heart Journey™ – "Understanding the Process"?

Greetings, Dear New WJH Community Member!!

If you are reading this section, you have probably just signed up for the Whole Heart Journey Community, or are considering becoming a participant in a group beginning in your area. Perhaps you are working through the materials as part of a class in ministry training. Whatever your reason, I pray Father God's wisdom & blessing upon you, as you seek to grow in the love and grace of our Lord Jesus.

You are headed into an adventure!!

The Whole Heart materials began as a ministry program which our church fellowship offered once a year, in the church my husband, Bill, and I pastor together. The videos, lessons, charts and worksheets are a culmination of my experiences as a counselor to families, couples and individuals, over the past forty years. And, as it turns out, this has been somewhat of an adventure for me, as well. I never thought I would be working in-depth with real people, with real pain, and heart-rending stories. It is always amazing how God truly works in His mysterious and amazing ways.

Forty-five years ago, when Bill and I began in ministry together, I didn't realize where the pastoring, counseling and healing ministry we began together would take us. Over the years, it has become evident that the majority of the people with whom we come into relationship, have been and are always still drawn by the Holy Spirit. Much of the time, we have encountered the same common denominator in each relationship --- the factors of a bruised will, and a broken soul.

In the corporate congregational setting, in gatherings for worship and group discipleship, that was a good thing… For the most part, these persons were kind, open, and caring. Each one was a solid participant, and some would become

involved in a service of one sort or another. But sadly, when a relational difficulty would arise in the course of serving, each one would become affected by the conflict at-hand, and would retreat into an "emotional insulation" of sorts. This insulation, we found, eventually resulted in the person accommodating a hardening within their soul to the Presence of God. Then, because of the soul's hardness, Holy Spirit-life and Spirit-formation was categorized into a performance syndrome, based on "*doing*" the right thing – instead of "*being*" the right person.

Along with this difficulty, each of these persons was incrementally overcome by a sense of feeling trapped. In serving within the Body-life, even when offered the chance to "step down," or "take a break," more than 90% expressed they felt compelled inwardly to continue "on-task." But even though adamant in their "soldiering onward," these persons expressed a sensing of personal emptiness, accompanied by isolation, and an inability to experience God's Presence or hear the Inner Voice of the Holy Spirit. The inward sense to "stay on-task" had certainly not come from God.

That being said, most of these people maintained personal Bible reading, and attended fellowship gatherings. But the "dark cloud" remained; a continued and pervading sense that Joy was "just out of reach." And, in every case, there was no inward motivation or empowerment to change the dark sense of sadness clinging to the soul.

The third challenge: they also felt drained emotionally, even in stress-free settings. Another word for it? They felt hollow somehow.

Fourth; the aforementioned "emotional insulation" would become a newly evident lack-of-character quality. An inability to express, give, and truly receive unconditional love would show itself. Carefulness with a fear of true authenticity was unmasked. This resulted in a cycle of pain and frustration in the person's heart and mind.

As pastors, we would teach, reassure, counsel, encourage, and spend our own energies to help these persons come to a place of consistency and security. Frustratingly, an underlying fragility remained; continually speaking brittleness in the person's day-to-day relationships. We found ourselves increasingly needing to give out more and more, sometimes to the point of repeating simple instructions to persons older than ourselves, wondering what we were "doing wrong."

The truth was hard to realize. These members of our congregation were finding it difficult to discover a healthy pattern for living through daily life events. They needed help on a human level – and even though we had education, we found ourselves tempted to "refer them to a professional."

But God….. (Ephesians 2)

The Holy Spirit kept nudging our hearts when we would pray – was there something we were missing in our efforts to "do ministry?" As we allowed the Holy Spirit to slow the pace, we began to finally grasp what it means to really disciple another person…. To work as under-shepherds with the Chief Shepherd to restore the human soul.

The pathway into true and lasting discipleship could only be entered through the surrender and healing process. Further…. Over the years, we observed the problem was not always demonic in nature (although much of the time the demonic influenced the person). In more than half of these people, the problems were based in emotional pain. That pain, along with poor parental imprinting and/or damaged bonding, had left individuals who had never received a solid foundation for healthy resilience or stability. There was no understanding of "how" to support the weight of relationships and/or tasks in the long-term. Further, beyond fulfilling task responsibilities, the majority of these men and women had issues with personal vulnerability and trust. Many insulated themselves into a busy life-style, allowing no connection or real heart-to-heart community – even within a church setting. (Some of these would say "*especially* within a church setting!")

These men and women just found *life difficult.*

As our ministry journey has continued, we have learned that every believer comes into the Presence of Jesus in need of healing. We are each on a journey called "life." In this journey, we each discover missing links in our own personal development. This happens to everyone.

Our responses determine our choices. Our choices determine our future.

In our experience, the presence of some sort of "missing link" seems to be the same. The *weapons* used by the enemy of our souls to bring about the pain or trauma in the first place can be *different.* But the *result* is always the same. We experience a sense of alienation from God. The wounds we bring into our new spiritual family need cleansing, mending, and healing; whether verbal abuse, emotional abuse, neglect, war, hunger, abandonment, rape, sexual abuse, molestation, alcoholic/addicted environments, divorce, or any number of other armaments in Satan's arsenal.

This experience is not limited to just the few.
The experience is shared by everyone who encounters new life in Christ.

(Stop reading here, and watch the next video segment.)

Statistics Section. Here are some statistics to help you to see how widespread these situations have become in our world's culture.

a. 55%-70% of every church in every ethnicity in the world consists of women. That means more than half of all congregations are female.

b. 80% of persons feel inadequate to make decisions that affect their own lives and the lives of others on a deep level. Many just accept everything that happens in a passive manner.

c. 89% or more of persons worldwide have some form of dysfunction they perceive has stymied them in their development to any kind of destiny, perceived or unknown.

d. 70% of women, and 65% of men, deal with depression, whether chemical or hormonal, triggered by inner life issues. The same is true of 55% of children/teens.

e. 75% or more of women *in the church* have experimented with drugs, alcohol, the occult, or sexual immorality, the scars of which have not been addressed on a deep level.

f. 3 in 5 *or more* of women worldwide, (and in the church), have experienced sexual abuse, physical abuse, or molestation before the age of 15. (We say "or more" because those statistics address the reported cases. The statistic is 1 in 4 for men.)

g. 88% or more of humankind have chosen to protect themselves with defensive mechanisms. These persons hold anger and distrust toward authority figures; living fear, guilt and shame based. This reactive choice, spurs on a sense of attachment hunger; feeling emotionally removed or "left out" in most friend and/or familial-life situations.

h. 78% or more of all persons have experienced a negative imprinting of male or female authority, constituted by neglect, ignorance, abandonment, or abuse. Of these, *all* we have known in counseling and ministry settings have determined that their abuse indicated something about their own personal life purpose and value.

i. 68% or more of men and women have experienced divorce, separation or marriage failure. (Marriage failure occurs when a couple continues to live together without connection; without real love in the marriage.) There are no statistics available for persons who live together, whether heterosexually or homosexually, as the persons tend to be transient in relationships.

j. 63% or more of women have experienced abortion. Of those women in that 63%, more than half have experienced *more than one abortion.* Some abortions have been forced due to incest-based pregnancy, and/or sexual abuse. Some are parentally forced on a young girl due to status or class. Some women have been forced by law to limit the number of children they are allowed to have.

And yet,

k. 80% of Protestant churches and 100% of Catholic churches place only men in the top leadership roles, with little or no structured ministry in place to help persons to deal with their past issues, further reinforcing a fear of trusting authority figures in many persons. In these congregations, women are usually left to care for their own development, or to find a way to heal without church input. More commonly, when a vulnerable person happens to reach out for help from a ministering person of the opposite gender, temptation and/or accusation occur. This is especially true if a woman is seeking help from a male minister. If both individuals are carrying and accommodating the same type of pain and brokenness, the result for both individuals becomes tempted with sexual and emotional sin.

l. Approximately 65% of pastoral leadership in churches worldwide target men for ministry, while downplaying the needs of females in the congregation, as subservient, less important, or worse, "hormonal." As a result, the conclusion among many women is that they must "soldier on," never addressing their deep issues. Also, as a result, men become focused on advancing into leadership roles, rather than building-up and "feeding" the lives of the family they have at home.

m. Approximately 74% of pastoral leadership in churches worldwide are ill-equipped and will wait until crisis arises to address/offer help to men with emotional or addictive issues. *(Sadly, many of our churches have no plan or persons in place to provide help and guidance when a relational crisis erupts.)* Often, when the family/individual cannot afford professional therapy, a sense of deep hopelessness and shame settle over these men. As a result, many men struggle privately with anger, depression, alcoholism, addiction, pornography, no sense of identity or leadership, and feel lacking in "how to" be a godly father/husband.

n. In the last twenty years, there has been a 60% decline in church attendance among persons who used to attend regularly.

o. 40% or more of Protestant Christian persons communicate they feel inadequate to safely and effectively communicate and/or disciple others.

p. 60% or more of persons say they find it very difficult to connect or relate with other persons on a level deeper than surface communication. They also indicate they have not received preparation or training in their development; whether from parents, authority figures, or other leaders in their lives: to empower them to feel in touch with their deeper emotions and/or fears, or how to communicate. More than half of these persons are medicated for anxiety or depression, as well as other "disorders and syndromes." Diagnosis and medication have not brought solution. Prayer and conversation alone have *helped,* but not brought freedom to the depth or degree the person feels the need of help.

All of the men and women mentioned in these statistics have come to places in their life journey where it became difficult to **reconcile their experiences of past pain** with **feeling safe enough to address that pain with other people.** Sadly, in church settings, the focus many times became "putting the best foot forward," or "soldiering on" rather than pausing to contemplate and truly yield to the love of Father God.

Considering all of the persons listed above, there was a common denominator, running like a muddy stream...

These persons _all_ struggled with a sense of emptiness in their spiritual understanding – going "through the motions" without real joy or substance of Life; without a real and growing *relationship* with Jesus Christ.

What is the missing link? On a spiritual level, it is the absence of real and transforming spiritual power in our church environments. **On a human level, it is *the absence of the ability to truly bond with another human being*;** *the ability to give one's heart to another person, without reserve – without fear; without waiting for the "other shoe to drop," or "keeping your options open, just in case."*

The need for guidance and teaching; and what I have come to call "Gap Mentoring," is even greater. This is the cry of an orphaned heart: It is a deep need for the Creator's Community; for relationship; for discipling; for unconditional love and friendship.

The healing of such a problem must begin with us; the church leaders. It is what the Apostle Paul referred to as "equipping" in Ephesians 4:11-12. The word translated "equipping" is more than just teaching and classes one day or two days a week. It is *"Katarismos*" – a Greek medical term for "setting a bone, mending what's broken, bringing into health." This has more to do with one-on-one confidentiality and safe healing, than it does with dealing with large groups of people at one time.

And the needs are innumerable. Our world suffers from poor attachments, broken attachments, traumatic attachments, shame, depression and futility.

In some persons, the ability to bond was once present in early childhood, but has been broken by trauma. At other times, and sadly, what I have found to be more common: the ability to bond was never present to begin with, Or, at best, damaged bonding/attachment was provided with missing pieces.

(Stop reading here and watch the next video segment.)

Personal History Accounts Section. Consider these personal accounts, from persons we have worked with over the years –

- She was a latch-key kid, raised in a Christian home, by working parents, who were never emotionally available. She couldn't remember a time when she felt connected, even though she had always gone to church. Even now, she has few friends, even though she tries to be a kind person. She finds it difficult to trust other people with the issues closest to her heart.

- He thought his life was the same life everyone else had experienced. A gambling, angry, father who verbally abused him. A mother who left him to himself as a boy because she had to work outside the home. He grew into a narcissistic teen with a distrusting heart. As an adult, he and his wife could not communicate, and his wife had to get away due to his angry abuse.

- Her father was mentally ill, and her mother would bring "uncles" home, allowing the three-year-old daughter to witness sexual acts that should never be seen, even by adults. She became homosexual because of trauma.

- His father sold drugs and ran an illegal network of heroine distribution in a large city. The boy had seen too much "of the world" to be considered a seven-year-old. When his father went to prison, he had to fend for himself. His mother had to work two jobs. As an adult, he wonders why he has anger issues and cannot feel safe or communicate love with his wife.

- As a little girl, she looked out of an upper window and watched a man in black put a box in front of the neighbor's door and run away. A few minutes later her entire home was shaken as the neighbor's home exploded into flames. Debris flew into their home. War was upon them. Her family had less than 12 hours to run for their lives. They left everything they knew and carried only what they could load into a small car. They lived as refugees for several years before finding a home in a new country. She still has trouble sleeping. Now fully grown, she still feels panic when she encounters a man dressed in black.

- His mother and her boyfriend didn't want the children "stealing food," so they put a lock and chain around the refrigerator. The adults spent their time locked in the bedroom, sometimes with friends. The four-year old boy, and his six-year-old sister, would hear things from the bedroom beyond imagination. Such happenings became the "norm" of their existence. The two of them dug in the garbage for their parents' food scraps. They fell asleep on the floor whenever they became tired, without a blanket, or pillow, or comfort. They both remember television being a constant companion.

- She was sexually molested (or "groomed") by her father from the age of three. The relationship became fully sexual when she was eight. At ten, she told her mother about the incest. Her mother didn't believe what she heard was true. Then, the mother watched the father sexually violate the daughter, and said nothing, did nothing. Two forced abortions occurred before the girl married at an early age to get away from her family. She struggled to believe an Unseen Father could really love her unconditionally.

- His father and mother "just were never there," and he chose to fend for himself and his baby sister at the age of five. He remembers cooking and cleaning, changing diapers and washing clothes. He remembers making the decision to "not feel" and "not cry." Now, he struggles with sitting still. He feels driven to work constantly. He finds it difficult to stop or "shut off" working and allow himself to enjoy the relationships God has provided in the people around him.

- She was sixteen years old when she told her father she had a dream to go to college. Her father's response was to tell her she wasn't smart enough or good enough to pursue her chosen career. In anger, her father sodomized her and threw her out of the house without her belongings, during the cold, northern winter. Without clothing or money, she lived with her best friend's family for a few years. She struggled with a homosexual lifestyle for over 5 years, before coming to Christ. When she married, she chose a man who cheated on her with several women.

- His alcoholic father beat him with a metal belt buckle and belt when he told him he was hungry. Then, the boy and his hungry siblings were forced to stand and watch the father, as he consumed a steak dinner and threw the bones at the children.

- Her husband would keep her at home without a vehicle, control her activities, and expect sex each night. When she was too tired to give it to him, after caring for her two toddlers during the day, as well as a neighbor's child, he would rape her. As the children grew, she took a job. Her husband expected an account for her wages, her time, and even her telephone calls. She was not allowed friendships outside of her husband's family. This abuse was spiritualized, in the name of "biblical submission." She lived in a state of constant depression and fear.

- She was married for 1 day, when her new husband informed her, he was thousands of dollars in debt, She was forced to work 2 jobs while he worked part-time. His addiction was video games. His inability to manage money, and her inability to speak up for her own needs, caused a wedge between them which lasted for more than ten years. Neither of them could communicate their deep yearnings or needs, and eventually drew distant and silent, continuing the relationship feeling completely alone, rejected. Eventually, verbal, emotional, physical and sexual abuse were part of the pattern she and her children had to escape in order to feel a sense of safety.

- He was just a few weeks old, born to a teenage drug-addicted mother, and alcoholic father, The boy was born with an unrecognized neuro-cluster of issues in his brain. One day, the father was left alone to care for the baby, when the mother went to work. In a drunken state, the father was unable to fully care for the child. So, when the baby kept crying, the father threw the tiny human against a wall, causing greenstick fractures to 7 of his tiny ribs. Additionally, due to drugs and alcohol in his tiny system, the baby experienced convulsions, and seizures often as an infant. Taken from his parents at 6 months, he grew up with a deep sense of abandonment and not belonging. As he grew into adolescence, learning disabilities hampered his ability to memorize and remember information. He felt as though his birth had been some sort of mistake.

- Raised in a minister's home in a large city, she and her siblings took a backseat to ministry. The family home was daily filled with persons from the congregation in desperate need of solution for daily living. Her mother worked, and her father was always in his home office. She remembers carrying the weight of household responsibilities at the age of 7 or 8. She doesn't remember playing outside or activities with her parents. As an adult, she wants nothing to do with church, and is not sure she believes in God, except as a hard taskmaster.

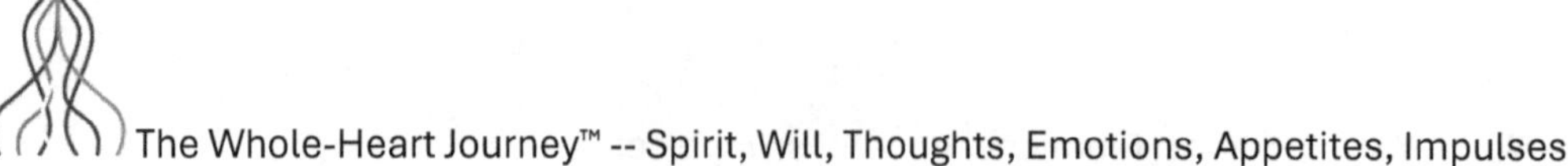

- While traveling with his mother and sister, he went to the men's restroom in a large airport alone. He was eight years old. A unknown man raped him and fled, leaving him bleeding, weeping, and afraid. The trauma of that event changed his ability to trust anyone. He struggled with pornography from that time forward.

There are so many other stories – perhaps yours is similar to the ones I have provided here. If that is the case, you need to know that God never wanted you to be treated in this way – He places more value on your life than other people have. He values you more than you value yourself.

Know this: **Jesus is still in the healing business** – and He knows exactly where you are – and what you need in order to come into deeper relationship with Him. He is preparing you for an eternal purpose – and He is doing that preparation right now.

Perhaps you have felt powerless in your ability to move beyond the level of spiritual life you are presently experiencing. This book and the group ministry of the Soul-Work Pathway Community will help you to discover key areas where you have become "stuck," or decided to just "quit hoping for more."

The fact you are reading this right now is a sign you didn't *really* quit – because you are considering a healing step right now.

Please understand. *Any* step you take will involve growth. And growth will always involve healing. Healing will bring change. After all, the root word in "healthy" is "heal." So, any journey into emotional and spiritual *wholeness,* will involve some sort of change – because *growth cannot happen without change* – just look at a child's student pictures from one year to the next. So, growth is healing, and healing means change.

And, isn't that what you are really hungry for? A safe and solid change?

Consider as well; *everyone on the planet is broken* – No one has arrived." Not one of us possesses the ability to heal ourselves. So… know this, **you are not alone in this place where you are.**

For more than forty-five years, Bill and I have worked in inner healing ministry. In this journey, there are two key principles we have learned:

1. **Maturity cannot be rushed, *and***
2. **Discovery cannot be forced.**

We have learned there is a need for any person seeking healing to *agree to take forward steps* in order to heal. We have also learned it is wise to establish guiding principles *to help the person receiving healing in focusing on the destiny Father God has for their lives.* When a group of persons meet together, and all are seeking healing from soul wounds, we have discovered the need for every person to become aware of how the pathway of healing progresses.

As a first step, it is vital to learn the basic operating system of the Kingdom of God; coming to awareness of what it truly means to live life in this realm as a follower of Jesus Christ. In so many situations over the past fifty years, I have come to a discovery mid-stride in helping another person who was caught or stuck in trauma recovery. Many times, the individual had never truly encountered the love of God or seen/experienced true love in action. This crucial foundation stone is universally needed for long-term healing to occur. For this reason, this class, "Understanding the Process" walks us each through the concepts of the Good News of Jesus, or the Gospel, and begins the journey of healing. This training is crucial for spiritual and emotional healing and growth. The problem is: most Christian believers in our day, have not learned the importance or even the Scriptural significance of their own lives, especially in the eyes of our Creator.

In this class, Understanding the Process, we utilize Four Cornerstone Concepts to define the boundaries, or "corners of the new building" the Holy Spirit begins to construct in a person's soul. For this class, these four concepts set boundaries for the foundational work we will be doing in this class, as well as during any/all additional classes during the rest of the Soul-Work Pathway program. This type of boundary setting is crucial for healing to begin. In fact, in my own counseling practice, I have become a firm believer in asking a client to sign a commitment for their own growth, and Inner Life Development. We call it a "Covenant Agreement," knowing that the Agreement serves as a reminder of the Lord's promises to *heal and seal* His work in that person's life later when the path can become hard or painful to continue. We use these same Cornerstone Concepts to begin the framework for The Soul-Work Pathway.

Here are the Four Cornerstone Concepts we utilize within this program. And, we have discovered over the years, we find ourselves continually coming back to these principles; in counseling between sessions, and in encouraging each other when Fear and Pain became the most strident voices within the soul. The Cornerstones are:

1. I choose to **move forward**
2. I choose to **serve**
3. I choose to **become a safe person**
4. I choose to **allow others into my life,** with humility and vulnerability

In this learning journey, we have discovered that the Pillar Principles (sessions six and seven of this Initiate level) are vitally important. When a member reaches a "hard place," or stumbles over a "rock in the road" these Pillars (or choices) provide a renewed grounding, or reminder, of a participant's determination to "choose to learn and grow."

It is my deepest hope that as you work through these materials, that the Presence of Jesus and His Holy Spirit, will visit you, envelope you, strengthen and encourage you, breathe upon you, and heal your life.

He is the Healer. He is the Builder. He is the Restorer. He is always Trustworthy.
He loves you. And so do I.

Blessings on your journey!!

Debbye

(Please stop reading here, and watch the next video segment.)

Introduction Session
Homework Assignments

Your Participation -- Assignment #1 – Please take a highlighter, go through the entire Welcome Orientation letter you just finished. Highlight the experiences and feelings you most identify with. Make a list on this page of how those accounts from other lives could Relate to you and your life experience.

Your Participation -- Assignment #2 – Now, looking at the paragraphs you highlighted, or the phrases you resonated with, take a few moments to consider each one.

Please write a description here of *your inner sense of the environments/situations you remember when those identifying moments occurred? Write those descriptions on this page.*

My Present Personhood Perspective (My PPP)

Name ______________________________ *Date* ____________________

Please use the scales provided to answer the following questions. ***It is helpful to take a few moments with each question, and consider your "heart" answer,*** *rather than giving a quick "head" answer. In this way, you will be able to obtain a clearer reading of the state of your soul's health .*

Please rate the answer to each question, by circling a number/indicator.

1. **Am I happy with my life?**

Ecstatic & Thrilled — Content/Happy — Discouraged/Miserable

10 9 8 7 6 5 4 3 2 1 0

What areas of your life currently make you happy? Can you sit quietly, and consider a concept or idea without feeling somehow pressured into getting up and accomplishing a task? What evidences are present in your life to support your response? **Write your answer here.**

2. **Do people really like me?**

I have several relationships which bring value — My presence in most situations is just tolerated — Not really. What's to like about me?

10 9 8 7 6 5 4 3 2 1 0

How many close relationships do you currently have with people you fully trust to know the good and bad accounting of your life? List those individuals here. Who do you trust most, and who would you trust least? What causes you to respond with this answer? (Just one word per name please)

3. To what degree do you feel comfortable with your personal appearance?

I am stunning	My looks are acceptable for my age and life experience	I have several physical attributes which I really don't like.	I hate the way I look.

10 9 8 7 6 5 4 3 2 1 0

What evidence supports your answer? Write it here.

4. Does my family love me?

I am an unreplaceable member of an inseparable family community. There are reciprocal relationship investments from all members. I know I am loved and important.	I invest in In my family, but I have to "coach" others to show friendship or real care. Sometimes I am pursued, but not usually.	I feel drained of personal resource most of the time. I initiate, but it is not returned. I feel like a caregiver.	I have no one to really look out for me, or my welfare. I have to take care of my own needs.

10 9 8 7 6 5 4 3 2 1 0

How long have you felt this way?

5. Do I feel as though I have something to contribute to others?

I have an un-replaceable contribution to the lives I touch every day.	I feel reasonably satisfied that my life makes a difference.	I fulfill a function, but it's something anyone else could do.	I am only tolerated in presence and in contribution

10 9 8 7 6 5 4 3 2 1 0

What do you sense about your ability to bond with others as friends, in a trustworthy relationship? Did your family of origin communicate on a safe and trust based level?

6. Do I feel I am responsible to maintain the emotional state of those I care for?

They are responsible for their choices, and I am free from feelings of negativity.	I seek to live my life aware of their needs, but I don't try to "create" an optimum environment.	I am responsible for my family's (or friends) unhappiness, and I must see that the atmosphere in our lives is a happy one.	I live in fear of someone's anger or negativity, and I try to condition my life to avoid those responses.

10 9 8 7 6 5 4 3 2 1 0

Do you avoid difficult conversations, even if they are necessary? Do you feel blame or guilty when there is conflict happening around you?

6. Do I think Father God loves me?

I experience His love and relationship every Day	I know He does, but I don't feel anything.	How can He love me? Look at my life.	He doesn't care, and I don't either.

10 9 8 7 6 5 4 3 2 1 0

Please write a few thoughts about your answer here.

Introduction --"Digging in" Spiritual Assignment

1. Please use this page to keep track of your assigned reading for the next week.

Please read Psalm 103 each day.

Day one ______ Day two ______ Day three ______ Day four ______

Day five ______ Day six ______ Day seven ______

Notes regarding what you are discovering about the nature of God as you are reading.

____

____

____

____

____

____

____

____

Devotional Reading – Introduction Session

First Things: "Before……"

Before.
The first word is "before."

What does that word mean to *you?*
Before.

What happened before?

Before the sadness.
Before the pain.
Before the trauma.
Before the memory.

What was life like before those things? Was it better? Was it full of peace?

Take a moment to think. Go back a little further. What was the environment of life like on the day you were born?

Was God there? Was He interested in your life that day? Did He care?

Before.

Let's keep going.

Look at the generations that came before yours. Your parents. Your grandparents. How about the traditions and legacies laid down before *they* walked on the planet? What came before even those earliest of histories?

Let's take a little time. Keep considering.
How far back should we go?
Look back even more.

What came before even *those* "befores?" Let your heart and mind consider a deeper concept. What if we were to go back ***all*** the way before?

Before the Romans
Before the Persians.
Before the Babylonians.
Before Abraham.

What was it like to live a life on our planet before *those generations* were here?

Did people walk through the day and sleep through the night-times? Were they happy? Did they have everything they needed?

What would it have been like to live during the days of Noah's flood? Imagine watching a 550 year-old man build a massive boat in the desert for ninety years.

Was God there then?
Did it matter to Him?
What would it have been like to live in *that* environment?

Before the first rainfall.
Before the stars could be seen.
Before humankind worshipped the sun and moon.

Are any of these "befores" even relevant to our lives now? Does that history even matter in our day-to-day lives in this present era?

It might surprise you, just how much "before" actually does have to do with your life right now. At this moment; wherever you are; in whatever situation you are.

Before.
Before the first murder.
Before shame existed. Or fear.
Before Time began.
Before creation began.

Was God there then? What was that environment like?

Before.
Before the earth was formed.
Before Light came into being.
Before Light and Darkness were separated.

Before there was a concept of "nothing."
Before there was a concept of "empty."

Where did these things come from?

Before. Was God there?

It's a little mind-blowing to think about. Our human brains think in limited spheres. In our world, everything has to have a beginning and an ending. But it isn't that way with God. He has always been and will continue to continue.

When we consider the "before," we each become intuitively aware of something greater;

Someone greater.
Someone who has been there always.

Before the Beginning.

Infinite. Eternal. Limitless.
Deeper still. Greater still. Bigger still.
Without End. Always.

What would that environment be like?
That Depth of Boundlessness, dear friend, IS the Before.

He is taking us there, as we study together in this series.
Please read the following verses and make a few notes here of what discoveries occur to you.

"In the beginning, God created ....." (Genesis 1:1)

____

____

"He is the Alpha and Omega, the Beginning and the End."
(Rev. 1:8; 22:13)

____

____

"In the beginning was the Word, and the Word was with God, and the Word was God. He was in the beginning with God. All things were made through Him, and without Him nothing was made that was made." (John 1: 1-3)

____

____

"He is the image of the invisible God, the firstborn over all creation. For by Him all things were created that are in heaven and that are on earth, visible and invisible.... All things were created through Him and for Him. And He is before all things, and in Him all things hold together." (Colossians 1:15-17)

____

____

Please memorize our memory verse for this Introductory Session:

> **Jeremiah 29:11**
> **"For I know the plans I have for you," says the Lord; "Plans for good and not for evil; plans for a future and a hope."**

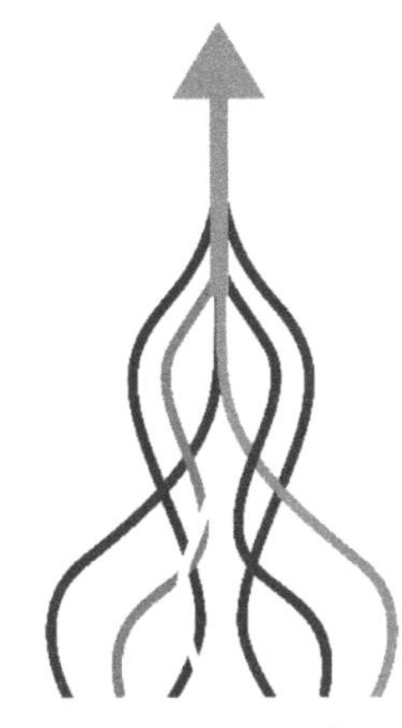

Spirit, Will, Thoughts, Emotions, Appetites, Impulses

The Whole Heart Journey™ –

"Understanding the Process"

Initiate Level Workbook

Session One - "The Open Place"

(Before beginning this session, please read the Devotional segment, "First Things: Open…." And complete the short Bible study attached.)

Devotional Reading – Session One

First Things: "Open......."

Open.
The next word is "Open."

Imagine, if you will, a wide expanse around you with no limitations, no boundaries. A weightlessness; with an absolute freedom to stretch as far as you possible can. What would it feel like to move about in that available area; to fly; to just rise up? Then to go higher? Reach farther? Even beyond? To just keep going with no end?

When we consider the idea of a place of "open-ness," where there is no beginning or ending, we cannot help but become aware of an unseen realm; outside of our present existence. A place filled with substance, yet without any sense of emptiness. A place of peaceful awareness, with an absence of conflict or alone-ness. In this open and endless environment, there is no time, no rejection, no disapproval.

What would we be describing?

At the very least, it would be a place every one of us would like to experience, isn't it?

Is it possible?

This place; with this description in mind, would be a place where pure Love dwells; where Safety and Security are in prominence. Where Peace rules. Where Peace and Power connect, and there is no conflict.

Right?

And if those things are true, then this would be a Spiritual place; where God dwells. In fact, this atmosphere actually describes the Presence of God; or the environment of Heaven. And, in totality, that environment is the expression of God's Personality and Attitude.

What would it be like to experience that kind of environment? What would it be like to live in that place on a day-to-day basis? Or encounter that atmosphere inside of yourself; in your emotions and thoughts?

This is the environment you became a part of when you chose to become a disciple of Jesus Christ. You were spiritually "born again." You became, in the core of your life, a spiritual being. An eternal person.

When we consider Who God truly is.... The eternal "I Am," we become aware of His Substance of Being. Just Be-ing.

Consider: To reach out with your inner yearnings; to take hold of the open space before you. Allow your heart to open it's pensive door. Step in to encounter the Real and Living God. There is no fear here. Only Grace. Only Healing. Only a Loving Creator who formed your life for a purpose.

Please read the following verses, and make a few notes here of what discoveries occur to you regarding the personality and character of God.

"The Lord is......." (Psalm 103:8-15)

____

____

"The fruit (or personality) of the Holy Spirit is...." (Galatians 5:22-23)

____

____

"By this we know God....." (I John 4:7-16)

____

____

"Where do we experience God? In what part of us?" (Revelation 3:20; Luke 12:34; Psalm 119:11)

____

____

The Whole Heart Journey ™ Understanding the Process

Session One –
"The Open Place"

(Please begin watching the Video session for Session One here. Write notes below)

What is an N.D.E.?

What is an environment, or atmosphere?

Genesis 1:1-2

  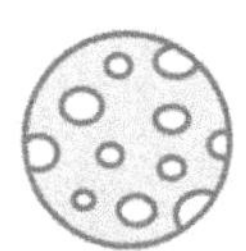    

What/Who is God?

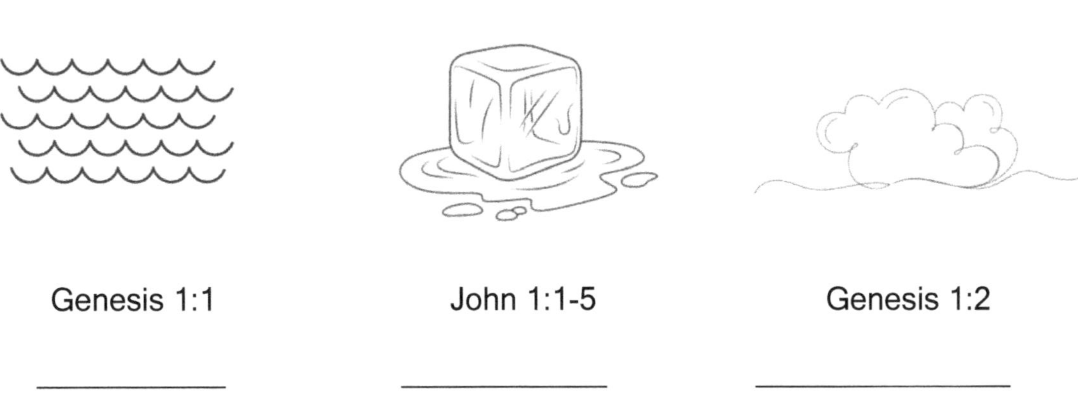

Genesis 1:1 ____________ John 1:1-5 ____________ Genesis 1:2 ____________

(Please work through these Scriptures as the Video continues, with the music, doing the written work.)

What do these Scriptures teach us about the Presence of God?

Job 38:4-11 ____

Revelation 4:2-11 ____

Psalm 16:11 ____

Isaiah 6:1-4 ____

____

(Please continue the video here, and use the following illustrations to help you with your notes.)

Psalm 90:2

Genesis 1:26

Genesis 2:7

John 1:18

John 14:9

What Does it Mean: The Presence of God?

In sociology, the "Power of Presence" is considered to be the "quality in a person's character. It is determined by the type of impact someone has on other people, due to their manner of BE-ing. BE-ing is defined by the person's ability or desire to inspire (bring life to), to connect with (through words of actions). The non-verbal cues or body language (expressions or deeds) of a person's attitude and demeanor are also important. People who are fully present with others practice BE-ing completely available in the present moment. Others remember persons such as this to have instigated the feelings of being seen, heard and given value.

What is the Nature of God?

When we think and learn about God, we discover Who He is (BE-ing) in the following ways:

1. What He says about Himself in the Bible.
2. What others have said about their true experiences with/in Him
3. What we read about Him, and learn from classes or lessons, helping us grow in Truth.
4. What we sense and inwardly understand from our own encounters with the His Holy Spirit.

(Please work through the following Scriptures as the Video continues, with the music, doing the written work.)

What do the following Scriptures teach us about the Essence, or Nature, of our Creator, who is God?

a. I John 1:1-5 ____

____

b. Psalm 103:8____

____

c. Galatians 5:22-23____

____

d. I John 4:1-18 ____

____

e. Hebrews 13:8 and John 3:17____

____

(Please continue the video here, and use the following illustrations to help you with your notes.)

What is an Open Heaven?

When the Bible refers to an "Open Heaven," the meaning is that God's presence and blessing, or "favor" is accessible and available to us who are living in this physical realm. This is a common occurrence in the Scriptures, and the New Testament teaches that Jesus came so that each of us can experience the reality of an "Open Heaven" in our lives on a day-to-day basis.

a. Genesis 28:10-17

b. John 1:43-51

(Matthew 3:15-17 & Luke 3:21)

c. Acts 7:54-56

(Ephesians 1 - *"epouraneos"*)

d. Revelation 4:1

e. Acts 10:11

f. Revelation 19:11

(Adam, Noah, Enoch, Abraham, Jacob, Moses, Joshua, Isaiah, Elijah, Ezekiel, Daniel, 3 Hebrew young men in a furnace, Samuel, David, Mary, Zachariah, Saul/Paul, Stephen, Peter, James the Greater, John the Revelator.)

(Please work through the following Scriptures as the Video continues - with the music, doing the written work.)

What are the Qualities of An Open Heaven?

a. I John 4:16-18____

____

b. I Corinthians 13:4-7_______________________________________

____

c. James 3:17-18____

____

(Please continue the video here.)

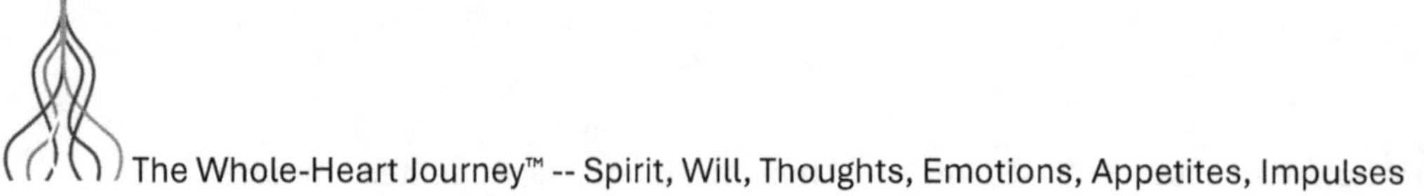

Session One --"Digging in" Spiritual Assignment

1. Please use this page to keep track of your assigned reading for the next week.

Please read Psalm 91 each day.

Day one ______ Day two ______ Day three ______ Day four ______

Day five ______ Day six ______ Day seven ______

Notes regarding what you are discovering about the nature of God as you are reading.

____

____

____

____

____

____

____

____

Please memorize our memory verse for this First Session: Psalm 103:8

"The Lord is gracious; full of compassion; slow to anger and great in mercy."

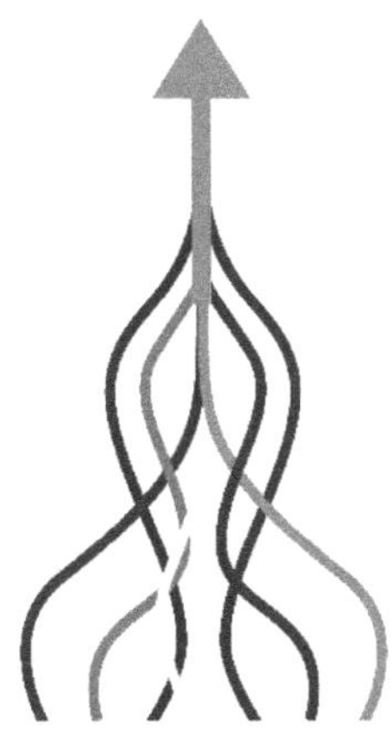

Spirit, Will, Thoughts, Emotions, Appetites, Impulses

The Whole Heart Journey™ –

"Understanding the Process"

Initiate Level Workbook

Session Two –

"The Betrayal of Darkness"

(Please begin this session by reading the Devotional segment, "First Things: Outside…." And completing the short Bible study attached.)

Devotional Reading – Session Two

First Things: "Outside......."

Outside.

The final word *could* have been "Outside."

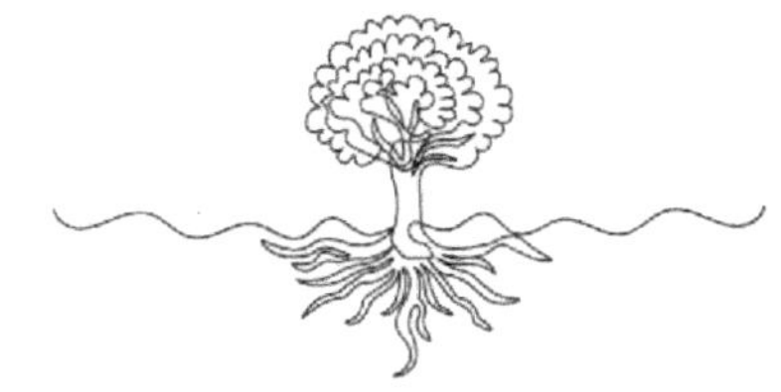

In the beginning, there was no "*out*-side." Everything created was *in*-side and wanted to be there. In Safety. In Security. In Community.

Loved. Wanted.

Designed. Down to the tiniest detail.

The out-side had to be created now. It was necessary to make space to put the "NOT" into place. No one else had seen it coming.

Before, there had been no conflict. Now, because of Love, there had to be a boundary given. A limit made. A line drawn.

A definition of Good had to be provided. And of the "NOT Good." The "Not *God*."

Oh, the Resistance had taken time. It had begun as just an idea, really. From the most beautifully crafted of them all. He had planted seeds of doubt in their minds. Most resisted his rumors; but then, his questions began to gain momentum.

They had reappropriated the gifts the Creator had built into their beings differently than had been designed. And, as a result, the Resistance had assembled quite a following.

The Shining One, the beautiful one; he had done it. Quenched it into being. Those who were less than he had begun to believe they could become stronger than their Creator. That one had told them he was better. Just stronger than God, after all.

This whisperer had taken time to tempt them into supposing...
And then had used deceptive strategy to gather them as his followers...
The sequential erosion had enabled him to gain listening ears, and then feed them lies so they would think as he did.

The Creator sighed. Today, they had done it. Finally.

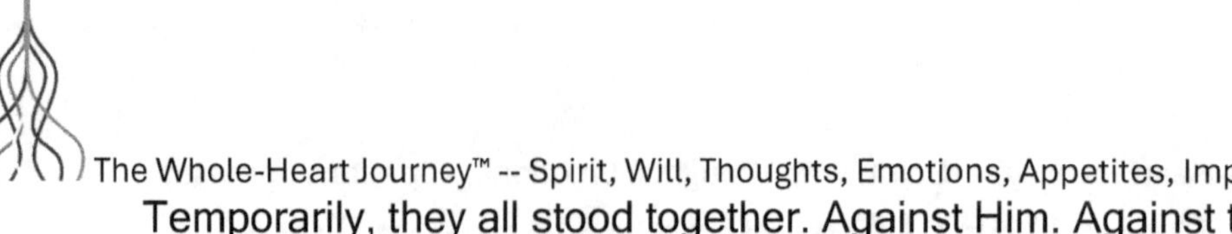

Temporarily, they all stood together. Against Him. Against the Good.

Against God.

"We want the 'Not Good!'" they cried. "We want something else! Something other than You! Some place other than You! We can do everything You can do! We want the 'Not God!' Your Presence is too limiting! We want more!"

Saddened, but not surprised, the Creator had seen it coming. He had watched them all along, sorrowed by their foolishness.

Where did they think their beauty and abilities came from? How could they become greater than the Source Who had given them Life?

In the end, the Out-side had been created to isolate it. Because of His Love for them, He enlarged a capacity for an existence outside of the Good. Outside of the God.

He separated the Light, which was Good ....

.... from the Darkness, which was Not Good.

For every *one* of them who stood with the Resistance, *two* had chosen the Good. These had stayed in Truth, and it had made them mighty!

The Resistance had even tried to fight, thinking they could usurp the very Throne of the Source of Life! It was unfortunate. They hadn't even realized until it was too late. They had, as a result, disconnected from the very Source of what they thought was their own power.

Now, all that remained was desolation. They were left with The Empty Place. The Abyss.

The opposite; the "Not-God."

The battle had not taken very long. After all, Love had been the Source of their strength. Unity had been their synergy. His Glory had been their beauty.

Stunned, the remaining two-thirds of the Open Place watched in silence. These had been part of the host, but now wanted nothing to do with the Creator?

The Creator levelled a steady gaze at the Shining One. He could see the Ambition is preening itself within him. It was a place of saddened understanding.

The Betrayal was complete.

"If you don't *want* to be in My Presence," he told them, quietly in great Love. "You *must* go. I will not force anyone to remain here who does not want to be. You have chosen."

The Company of the Resistance stalled in surprise. They had not expected to *fail.* They had believed the Shining One. He had told them God would be forced to do their bidding.

.....That the Throne would be *theirs.*

But that was not to be. At the end of the Creator's words, all of the beings participating in the Resistance were suddenly falling.... then enveloped in a new environment. It was the OUT-side.

The Darkness.
The Empty.
The Fear.
The Division.
The Pride. The Quest for more.

Immediately, according to their varied sizes and strengths, they each began to clutch and claw against each other, fighting for supremacy.

For Dominance. Control. With Violence and Rage.

The upheaval and chaos became intolerable for their leader, the largest one of them all, who was no longer a "shining one."

"Stop!" he bullied, snarling. "We will have another opportunity."

Livid and grumbling, the fallen ones, slowly found isolation, each one alone in their own misery and hatred. Hating and vengeful, they could not stand the sight of each other.

Another opportunity? What did that mean?

Above, in the Open Place, the Creator could see them. And hear them.

He knew His betrayer. He had not been surprised. Truth could not accept any Lie.

Choices had been made.

And, because He could see the destruction being schemed.

The Creator already had a Plan in place.

Considering the devotional text, please read the following verses, and make a few notes here of what discoveries occur to you regarding the personality and character of God.

"We give thanks to the Father because....." (Colossians 1:12-14)

____

____

Who is Jesus Christ? (Colossians 1:15-18)

____

____

Who is the deceiver? (Revelation 12:9)

____

____

What does the Word teach about our relationship to God when we experience difficulties in our lives? (Romans 8:38-39)

____

____

The Whole Heart Journey ™
Understanding the Process

Session Two –

"The Betrayal of Darkness"

(Please begin watching the Video session for Session Two here. Write your notes below)

Last session, we discussed the Open Place, or the Presence of God. What must it have been like to be present during the process of Creation?

Revelation 4:2-11

Genesis 1:1

Genesis 1:2

Genesis 1:3

John 1:1-13

I John 1:1-5

(Please work through the following Scriptures as the Video continues - with the music, doing the written work.)

1. What does Revelation 21:23 teach us about the Source of Light?

____

2. What does Colossians 1:15-17 teach us about the seen (natural) and the unseen (spiritual) realms?

(Please continue watching the video here. Write your notes below)

Psalm 80:1 and Exodus 25:8-22

Ezekiel 28:12-17

Isaiah14:12-15

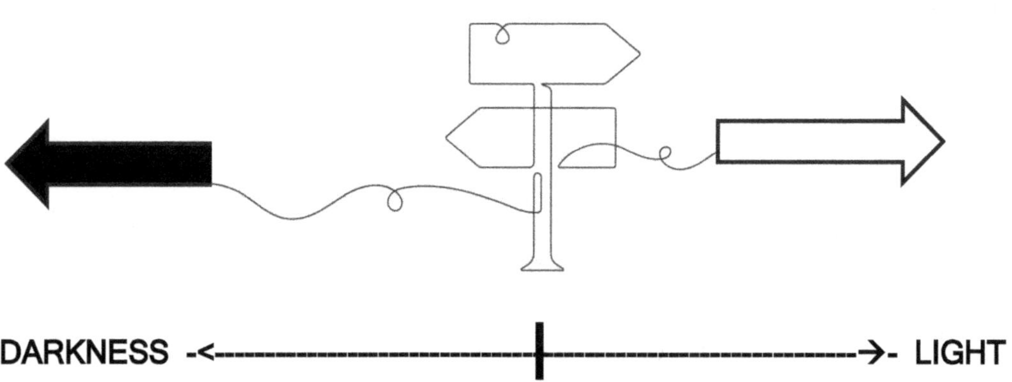

DARKNESS -<------------------------------------|------------------------------->- LIGHT

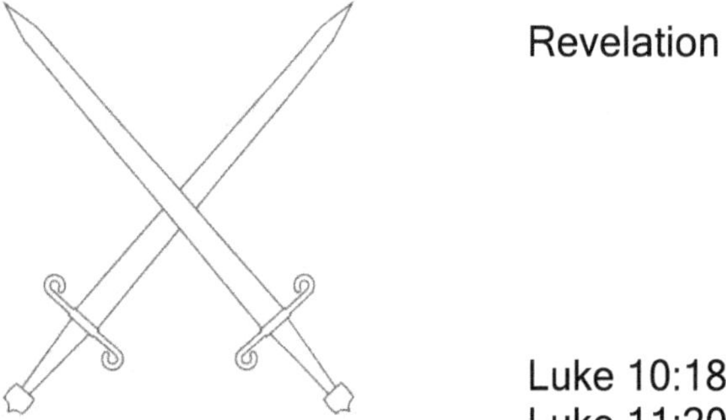

Revelation 12:7-9

Luke 10:18
Luke 11:20

Genesis 1:4–what does this verse mean in our lives as believers? How does God still do creative work in us to separate His Light from the darkness? (See II Corinthians 5:17)

Session Two --"Digging in" Spiritual Assignment

1. Please use this page to keep track of your assigned reading for the next week.

Please read John 1 each day.

Day one ______ Day two ______ Day three ______ Day four ______

Day five ______ Day six ______ Day seven ______

Notes regarding what you are discovering about the nature of God and His love for you as you are reading.

____

____

____

____

____

____

____

____

Please memorize our memory verse for this Session: Psalm 34:18

"The Lord is close to the brokenhearted, and saves those who are crushed in spirit."

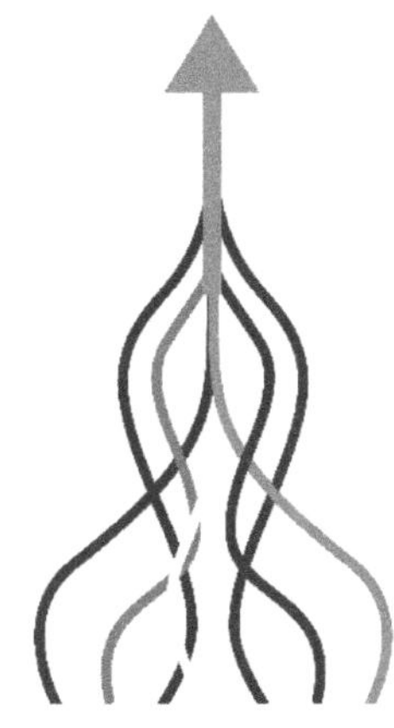

Spirit, Will, Thoughts, Emotions, Appetites, Impulses

The Whole Heart Journey™ –

"Understanding the Process"

Initiate Level Workbook

Session Three –

"The Eternal Synthesis"

(Please begin this session by reading the Devotional segment, "First Things: Indescribable...." And completing the short Bible study attached.)

Devotional Reading – Session Three

First Things: "Indescribable...."

There are no words, really. How would you describe the
color blue to a blind man? How would you communicate the
meaning of "sunlight" and all that is contained
in just that one word?

To be completely aware of who God is....
To be fully known,
Fully accepted.
With absolute approval.

With no hint or knowledge of what it even means to be Rejected or Alone.
Unhindered.
Fulfilled.
Confident.
Unaware of Evil.

Can you imagine? What would that feel like? What would it look like?
To be able to see into the eternal realm,
To utilize all of your brain and sense of emotion?
To be fully present and alive?
To remember, and know?

To see and speak with God.....
..... to see and speak with angels....
.... to speak with the animals....

In a climate-controlled environment, where not even clothes were needed for warmth or comfort. Food within reach. Entirely satisfied. Altogether content.

Naked.	Without Shame.
Innocent.	Without Regret.
Centered.	Without Distraction.
Beautiful.	Without Pride.

This was how Life began. In a Garden. Lush and green; without weeds, or even hardness of soil. All that was required was ....
that Adam, male and female,
would cultivate it, would tend and keep it....
But mostly.... They would *Enjoy it.* Together.

Every day, they walked and talked with their Creator, getting to know Him in the early morning; the coolest time of each day.

Together. With each other.
Together. With God.
Together. With Creation.

And all the while....

In the shadows, in the stillness of the night, as Adam, male and female rested, Lucifer waited. The former cherubim, now a dragon and shapeshifter, lay in wait.

"It's only a matter of time," he sneered silently. "I will become their god. I can make them want what I want; the *not*-God. I even have the bait now."

In preparation, the dragon preened himself as he connived.

It was all too easy; he would yet take the Throne.

Considering the devotional text, please read the following verses, and make a few notes here of what discoveries occur to you regarding our Creator's design for us as His image-bearers,

What does Ephesians 3:10-12 say was God's intention when He created us?

____

____

What are the main tactics Lucifer (Satan) uses against humankind?

Matthew 4:1-11 ______________________________

Revelation 12:10______________________________

I Peter 5:8 ______________________________

Revelation 12:9 ______________________________

2 Corinthians 4:4 ______________________________

John 10:10 ______________________________

The Whole Heart Journey ™

Understanding the Process

Session Three –
"The Eternal Synthesis"

(Please begin watching the Video session for Session Three here. Write your notes below)

What is "Synthesis?"

In science, the word synthesis is used to describe the process taking place when two or more separate things are combined, or bonded. to create an entirely new element.

Only open molecules can bond.

Genesis 1:1-3

Malachi 3:6

Psalm 90:2

(Please work through the following Scriptures as the Video continues - with the music, doing the written work.)

1. What was the purpose of Creation, according to the following Scriptures?

Isaiah 46:10 ____

Psalm 19:1-6 ____

____

(Please continue watching the video session here. Write your notes below)

The Order of Creation

Gen. 1:1-2	**The Beginning – Heavens and the earth**
Gen. 1:3	**Day One – Light; separated the Darkness**
Gen. 1:6	**Day Two – The Sky; separated the waters**
Gen. 1:9-13	**Day Three – Dry Land and seas; grasses fruit, and trees**
Gen. 1: 14-19	**Day Four -- Sun, moon, stars, seasons, Cycles of weather**
Gen. 1: 20-23	**Day Five – Fish, sea creatures, birds**
Gen. 1: 24-31	**Day Six – Land animals and Adam (male and female in one being.)**
Gen. 2:1-2	**Day Seven – God rested**

The overview of the Creation account is given in Genesis 1.

Then, in the traditional story-telling style of the ancients, more details of the overview are provided in Genesis 2.

Foundation Truths.

Colossians 1:13-17

"Ex Nihilo" ---

"Ex Materia" ---

What is Laminin?

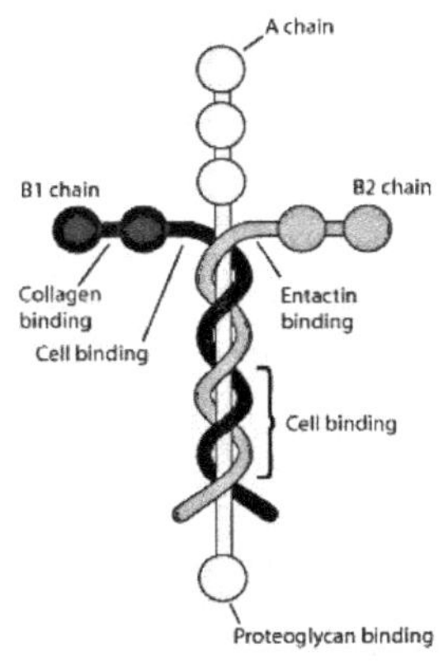

What is Lignin?

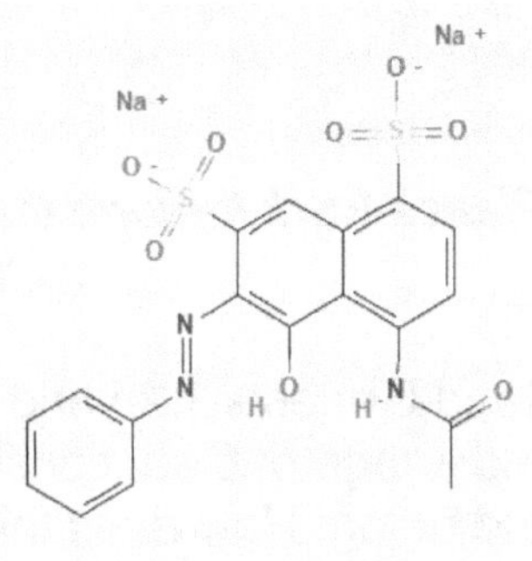

Let's Put Some Pieces Together

Genesis 1 and Genesis 2 -

"Made in the image of God"

What did it mean to be like Adam? To have relationship with God, in God's Environment; the atmosphere of Heaven?

Imprinting

Conscience

Designed Purpose

(Please work through the following Scriptures as the Video continues - with the music, doing the written work.)

2. Read Genesis 1:26 and Genesis 2:18-25. When Adam was first created in the likeness and image of God, consider these accounts indicate that he was male and female in one being. How does this concept translate for you personally, regarding God being able to relate to us as both Father and Mother as our Creator?

____

3. In Genesis 3:8, the Scripture indicates that it was a normal daily activity for Adam to walk and talk with God in the cool of the day. What value does this verse indicate to you that God places on walking and talking with His creation?

____

4. What purpose and position was Adam (male and female) given over the planet called "Earth?" Please list the actions listed Genesis 1:28, Genesis 2:5, Genesis 2:8,

___

___

(Please continue watching the video here. Write your notes below)

Genesis 2:15-17

Genesis 2:18-25

What does "Eternal Synthesis" really mean?

Mark 8:31

John 3:5-21

Matthew 17:22-23

Daniel 7:13-14

Matthew 25.31

Matthew 20:28

Revelation 14:14

When God Plants a Garden

Session Three --"Digging in" Spiritual Assignment

Please use this page to keep track of your assigned reading for the next week.

Please read Colossians 3 each day.

Day one ______ Day two ______ Day three ______ Day four ______

Day five ______ Day six ______ Day seven ______

Notes regarding what you are discovering about the nature of God as you are reading.

____

____

____

____

____

____

____

____

Please memorize our memory verse for this Session: 2 Corinthians 4:7

"But we have this treasure in earthen containers, so that the extraordinary greatness of the power will be of God, and not from ourselves."

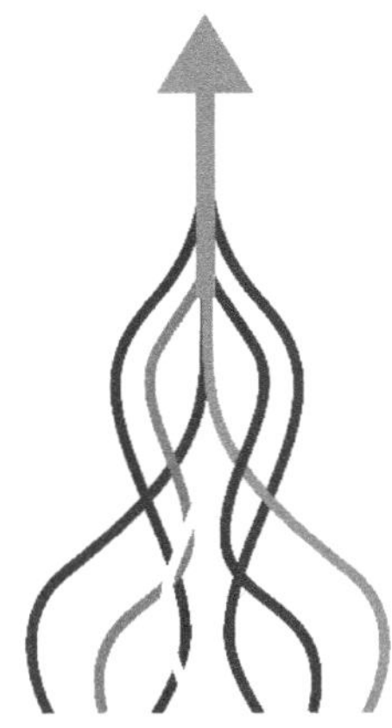

Spirit, Will, Thoughts, Emotions, Appetites, Impulses

The Whole Heart Journey™ –

"Understanding the Process"

Initiate Level Workbook

Session Four –

"The Broken Spirit"

(Please begin this session by watching the Devotional Video, "The Ponder Principle," and completing the short Bible study attached.)

Devotional Mini-session/Video – Session Four(a)

First Things: "The Ponder Principle"

What is the PONDER Principle?

"But Mary kept all these things, and pondered them in her heart." Luke 2:19

(Please begin watching the devotional video here.)

P -- We **PAUSE**, meaning we stop thinking about other things, and we give our full attention to the concept being considered.

What do these scriptures teach us about taking a pause from our day-to day mindset, and placing all of our focus on the realm where God is found?

Colossians 3:2-4
____

____

Romans 8:6 ____

____

(Please pause your written work to watch the video here.)

O --We **OBSERVE,** meaning we look at what is being taught from an objective viewpoint. What do these scriptures teach us about our need to consider making a change to keep our thoughts and hearts in alignment with the Word of God?

Deuteronomy 12:32____

____

Proverbs 23:12 ____

____

(Please pause your written work to watch the video here.)

N --We **NOTE,** meaning we make written notes of points & questions we have regarding what is being taught. What do these Scriptures teach us regarding the importance of keeping written records of what we sense the Holy Spirit is saying about our hearts?

Exodus 17:14 ____

____

Habakkuk 2:2-3____

____

Jeremiah 30:2____

____

(Please pause your written work to watch the video here.)

D --We **DECIPHER,** meaning we look at our written notes, and what is being taught, and find the Biblical truth regarding what is being discussed. What do these Scriptures teach us about becoming able to tell the difference between what is from God, and what is influencing our hearts from elsewhere? (the world, the devil, our past, our traditions)

II Peter 3:16____

____

II Timothy 2:7____

____

Colossians 2:8 ____

____

(Please pause your written work to watch the video here.)

E --We **EXCHANGE,** meaning, we yield or let go of any unhealthy or painful areas in our thinking and emotion, which would be defined as "our own truth and perceptions." We offer these perceptions for change. We choose to accept God's Truth over our own inner "survivor" choices... Psalm 51:6 tells us God "desires Truth in the inward parts" of our souls. This means we choose to agree with the healthy thinking provided by our Creator in His Word. We will touch on this more deeply in one of our sessions together. The practice of Exchange is crucial in our lives and growth as believers in Jesus Christ. What do the following Scriptures indicate is needed (on our part) in order to be equipped to live our lives in Truth?

John 8:32____

____

Colossians 2:6-8____________________________________

____

Psalm 51:6____

____

(Please pause your written work to watch the video here.)

R -- We **RECEIVE** forgiveness, healing, understanding and freedom to replace what we have yielded & offered as our living sacrifice. We choose to live our life in God, growing with unveiled face into the image & likeness of Jesus, growing from glory to glory, rather than from crisis to crisis. What do the following Scriptures teach us about yielding to the gentle direction of the Holy Spirit, to receive healing and change?

Psalm 51:6____

____

Ezekiel 36:26 ______________________________________

____

II Corinthians 3:18___________________________________

____

(Please pause your written work to watch the video here.)

Based upon the discoveries you have made from the Scriptures, please "ponder" and answer the following questions.

What do you sense the Holy Spirit ministering to your heart about the Ponder Process in your own life? What thinking patterns would you like to change? Make a short list here.

____

____

Are there relationships and responses in which you would like to learn to think with more positivity, and less negative expectations? Is your mindset about God influenced by these same thinking patterns? Write out your personal thoughts about how God probably feels about you.

____

____

The Whole Heart Journey ™
Understanding the Process

Session Four –
"The Broken Spirit"

(Please begin watching the Video session for Session Four here. Write your notes below)

Adam's Original Design

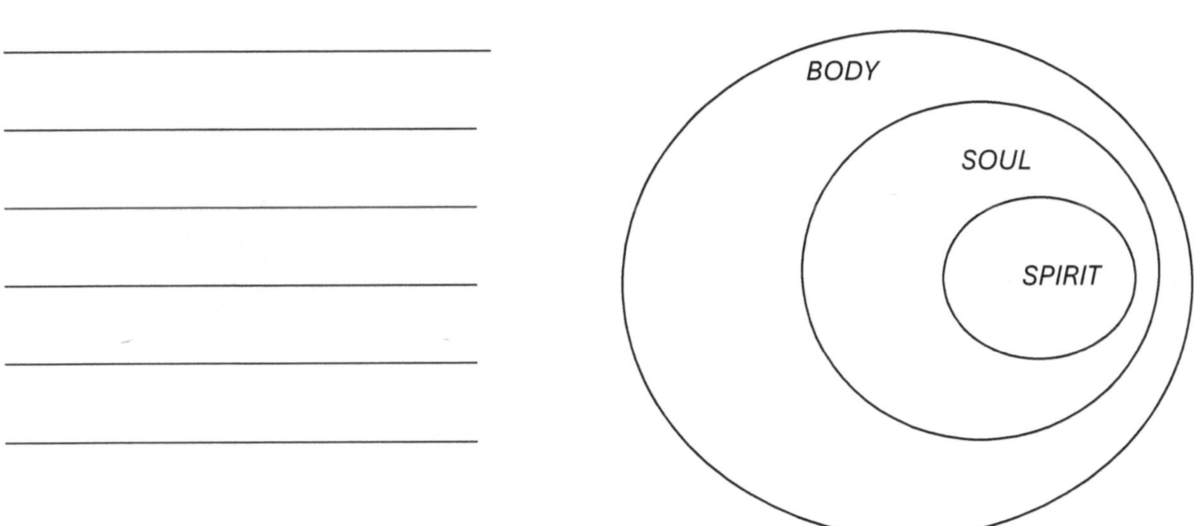

Each part affects the whole.

THE TABERNACLE OF MOSES

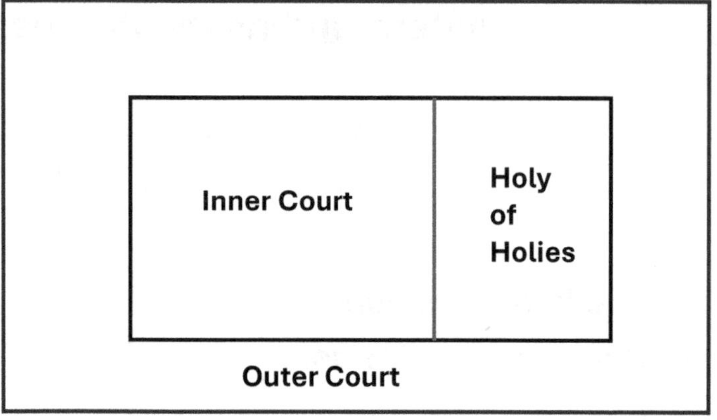

Hebrews 8:1-6 (*5)

Revelation 21:3-4

Tabernacle – Greek "skaynay"

The Original Design of Creation was that of Unity.

Unity is not identicalness or uniformity – or lack of uniqueness.

What Did Unity with God Look Like? Feel Like?

John 17:22-24

I Corinthians 6:17 ---- "Perichoresis"

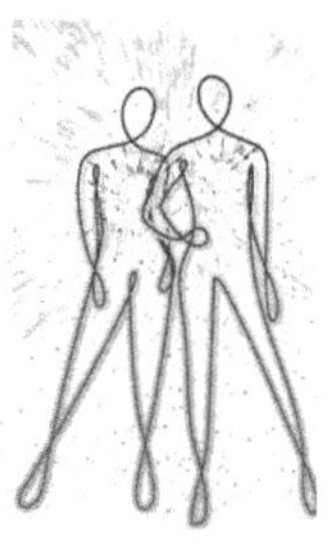

Genesis 2:25

Naked Vulnerability without Shame or Perceived Disapproval

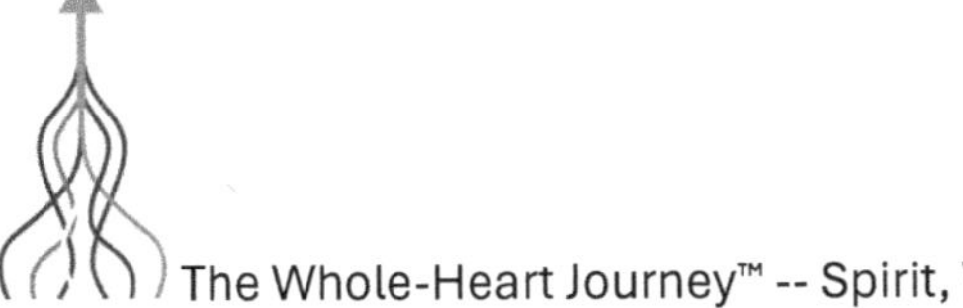

The Original Created Inner Flow of Adam's Being

He was Holy-Spirit Led

Before Sin entered the planet, man and woman were unaware; in a childlike state. They were innocent. Because they were unaware, they were naked, vulnerable, and had no reason to have secrets from each other. They could be easily known. They were completely trusting. They were full of motivation and excitement. Each day held expectation for Living.

CREATOR GOD's SPIRITUAL LIFE –
Confident communion with God and each other

↓

ADAM's SPIRITUAL LIFE –
Truth-based Perceptions and Intuition

↓

Healthy **Will** (positive choices)

↓

God-ordered **Mind**/Peace (thoughts)

↓

Whole and vigorous **Emotions**/Contentment (feelings)

↓

Healthy Appetites **(Body)** (unique preferences)

↓

Connection was part of the Created Need for Community

Holy Spirit-Led flows through humanity and provides the template for day-to-day living and relationships

(Please work through the following Scriptures as the Video continues - with the music, doing the written work.)

1. What do the following Scriptures teach us about how God's Spirit wants to flow through our lives?

   Genesis 2:7 ____

   ____

   Zephaniah 3:17 ____

   ____

   John 17:20-24 ____

   ____

(Please continue watching the video here. Write your notes below)

The Creator placed the man and the woman in the garden.

As representatives and stewards of His design and blessing in the Earth.

Genesis 3:1-3

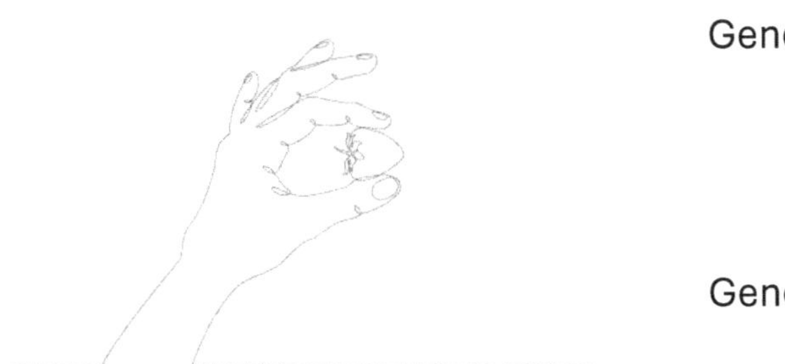

Genesis 3:4-5

Genesis 3:6

Genesis 3:7-8

(Please work through the following Scriptures as the Video continues - with the music, doing the written work.)

2. What do the following Scriptures teach us about the enemy's ability to tempt human beings?

James 1:13-15 ______________________________

I Corinthians 10:13 ______________________________

3. What does I John 1:15-17 provide as the world's elements of temptation?

1. ____(Genesis 3:6 good for food/taste)

2. ____(Genesis 3:6 pleasing to the eye/appearance)

3. ____(Genesis 3:6 made one wise/informed)

(Please continue watching the video here. Write your notes below)

What did Jesus teach us about spiritual life?

John 4:24

John 3:5-8

Because of the choice of the first Adam (male and female), the spiritual part of mankind died in the Garden.

Because of the choice of the last Adam (Jesus Christ), the spiritual part of mankind was provided the opportunity to be spiritually reborn.

The Problem with Fig Leaves......

Session Four --"Digging in" Spiritual Assignment

1. Please use this page to keep track of your assigned reading for the next week.

Please read Galatians 5:13-25 each day.

Day one ______ Day two ______ Day three ______ Day four ______

Day five ______ Day six ______ Day seven ______

Notes regarding what you are discovering about the nature of God and His love for you as you are reading.

____

____

____

____

____

____

____

____

Please memorize our memory verse for this Session: Colossians 2:8

"See to it that no one takes you captive through philosophy and empty deception in accordance with human tradition, in accordance with the [elementary principles of the world, rather than with Christ."

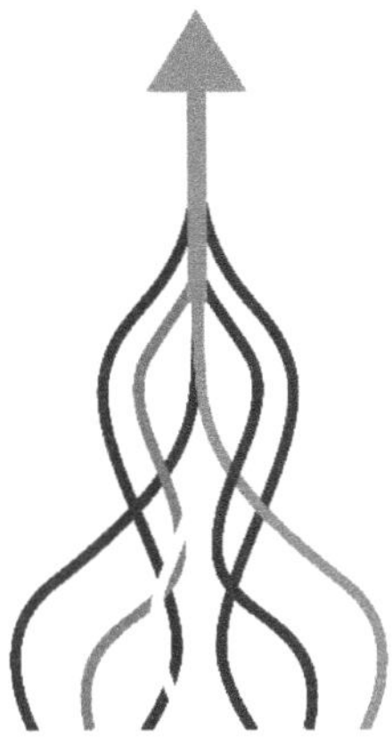

Spirit, Will, Thoughts, Emotions, Appetites, Impulses

The Whole Heart Journey™ –

"Understanding the Process"

Initiate Level Workbook

Session Five –

"The Limited Antithesis"

(Please begin this session by reading the Devotional Section, "First things…. Cheated," and completing the short Bible study attached.)

Devotional Reading – Session Five

First Things: "Cheated...."

The Creator had known they would have to choose. to be with Him, and become like Him, they would need to choose the Light.

The deceiver had no idea a Plan was in place; he just wanted power and control. Getting them to give him their allegiance; give away their delegated dominion.... That had been the goal. His end game.

So.... they had been cheated..... And now it was too late....

They hadn't even seen it coming..... so naïve.

To be truthful, had they been aware of the value of what they had been given to begin with, nothing would have ever been forfeited.

Not Ever.

But they *hadn't* known.

The whisperer had deceived them. He had been so sincere.... so convincing.....

And now the whispers were inside.

"You *should* have....."

They *would have* listened... heeded the warnings. Ignored the whispers.
Not believed him.
Not tried to answer the questions....

"You *could* have...."

"If *only*...."

Why hadn't they avoided going over there?"
Not listened to that voice....

Why had they even gone *close?*....

But.... His voice had made sense....

And the fruit had been so beautiful. So *fragrant.*

They hadn't thought it would hurt to *look* at it.... Or *touch* it....

But that one bite had changed everything.... Everything.....

Why had they *swallowed* it? Why hadn't they spit it out?

"It was her fault," the man thought.
"I wish he had stepped up, and said something," the woman thought.

But it was too late now. There was no going back...

The Music had gone away. The Light had gone away.
The atmosphere was different.... What was this feeling they suddenly shared?

They couldn't see anymore.... Or hear the music.....
The.....
the....
That sense of Glory was......

just gone.

Now there was NO Safety. *Anywhere.*

Now, they both were desperate, and..... uh... ...... well, ... afraid...
Inside, they felt.... Well, scattered.

They had to hide. To survive.

Survive? What did that even *mean*?

From his hidden vantage point, Lucifer the Betrayer watched his prey.

Now it was just a matter of time, until he had it all. They had been easy to trick, to sway, to deceive......

They would ask questions; he knew that. But now, he could fabricate lies, logic, answers, and they would hear him, with no interference. That part of them had died. He would need to strategize to get them used to living in the Darkness.

But now, they were In *his* environment.

He sneered in dark amusement. He had stolen control. The Creator had no clue what was coming..... Gaining domination had been too simple.

It was just logic from here.... Now, he could push the Pain button any time. He could prod them; drive them with Fear.

Had it been Innocence or Ignorance?

Curiosity or Cunning?

Deception or Decision?

The connection had been destroyed. Interrupted. Undone.
He hadn't created them...... but he could control them.... they had chosen.

Considering the devotional text, please read the following verses, and make a few notes here of what discoveries occur to you regarding our Creator's view of people who make mistakes and/or bad decisions?

Proverbs 28:13____

Proverbs 24:16____

____

Philippians 3:13-14____

____

The Whole Heart Journey ™

Understanding the Process

Session Five –
"The Limited Antithesis"

(Please begin watching the Video session for Session Five here. Write your notes below)

Genesis 1:26 – "radah" -- dominion

What were the after-effects of choosing?

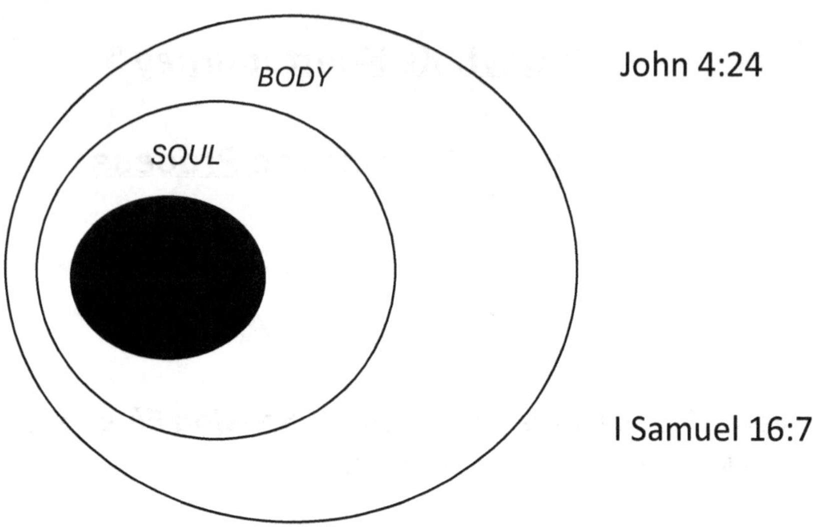

John 4:24

I Samuel 16:7

Genesis 2:17

I Corinthians 15:20-22

Genesis 3: 8-10

Genesis 3:11-12 (Proverbs 18:8)

Genesis 3:13

Genesis 3:14

Genesis 3:15

Genesis 3:16

Genesis 3:17-19

Genesis 3:20-21

Genesis 3:22-24

What Happened to the Man & Woman's Nature After they Chose?

Holy Spirit-Led

Leads	**human spirit**
Guides	**human will (choices)**
Directs	**thoughts(mind)**
Limits	**feelings (emotions)**
Disciplines	**appetites**
Confines	**impulses**

Fear Driven

Stresses	**human impulses**
Pressures	**human appetites**
Pushes	**feelings (emotions)**
Darkens	**thoughts (mind)**
Demands	**human will(choices)**
Shuts out	**human spirit (and The Spirit of God)**

CHOICE

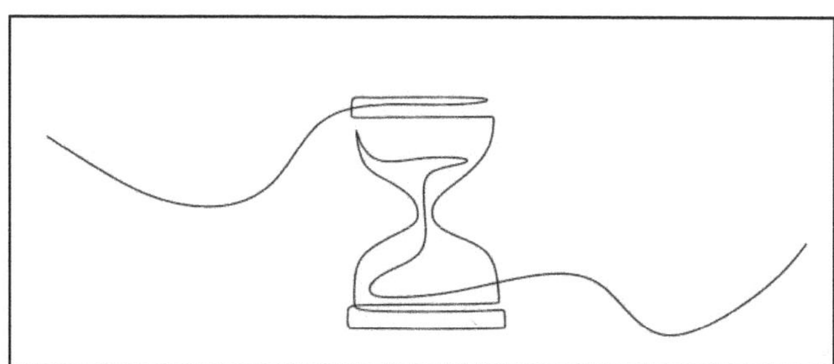

EXPERIENCES LIFE and PEACE

Romans 8:6

John 14:25-27

IGNORES the HOLY SPIRIT

I Thessalonians 5:19

Ephesians 4:30

(Please work through the following Scriptures as the Video continues - with the music, doing the written work.)

1. Looking at the comparison chart on the last page, consider your own experience in your personal development. Do you see a difference between how the Holy Spirit wants to lead in your life, and an area in your life where you may be reacting to an old life/pain/trauma (sin environment) learned pattern? Make a note of that comparison on the lines below.

____

____

____

____

Pondering this discovery, is there an experience or relationship you can connect with this difficult pattern of personal struggle? Make note of that discovery on the lines below.

____

____

____

____

(Please continue watching the video here. Please take notes as you watch below.)

Romans 8:12-17

The Battleground in the life experience of a

Jesus-follower is ______________________________

Philippians 1:6

Session Five --"Digging in" Spiritual Assignment

1. Please use this page to keep track of your assigned reading for the next week.

Please read Psalm 34 each day.

Day one ______ Day two ______ Day three ______ Day four ______

Day five ______ Day six ______ Day seven ______

Notes regarding what you are discovering about the nature of God and His love for you as you are reading.

____

____

____

____

____

____

____

____

Please memorize our memory verse for this Session: Isaiah 41:10

"Do not fear, for I am with you; Do not be afraid, for I am your God. I will strengthen you, I will also help you, I will also uphold you with My righteous right hand."

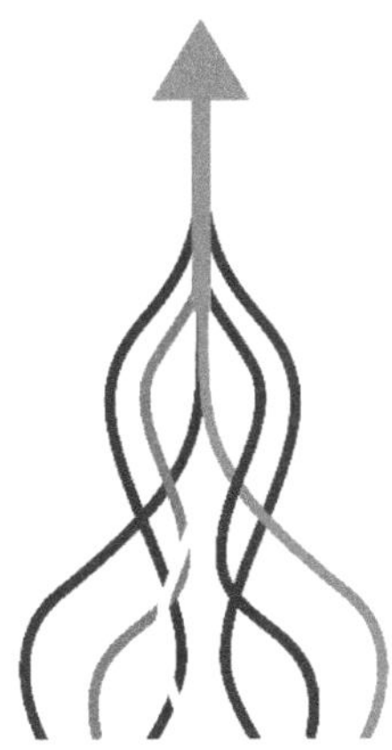

Spirit, Will, Thoughts, Emotions, Appetites, Impulses

The Whole Heart Journey™ –

"Understanding the Process"

Initiate Level Workbook

Session Six –

"The Spirit of Adoption"

(Please begin this session by reading the Devotional Section, "First things…. "Forward," and completing the short Bible study attached.)

Devotional Reading – Session Six

First Things: "Forward...."

How?

That's the question we ask most. Usually silently.

"How do I do this? What's the next step?"
After all, no one has a picture on the jigsaw
Box called "This Life on Earth."

Well, to be honest; we *do* get *a* picture.
But it's never the "Before."
It's never the "Perfect."

I don't know about you, but I definitely have had a few experiences in my life when I learned something; or when I saw something that I later wished I had never been exposed to.

You just can't *"un-see,"* some things.
Nor can you *"un-discover"* a negative fact or experience.

Why is it that difficult situations seem to have a way of affecting us multiple times afterwards, many times in our dreams, or, even causing reactions in our day-to-day experiences? Sometimes for years?

Why doesn't the soul heal on its own like our physical bodies do? Have you ever found yourself asking that question?

Because the soul is unseen; and parts of it are eternal.
The soul requires intentionality.
Of choice
Of thought
Of invested emotion.

We can't go back---- that would be like trying to put toothpaste back into the tube it came from. Or, re-attaching leaves after they have fallen to the ground in the fall season.

All we can, those of us who live life on the planet
in the "After" is choose to move forward.

Away from the darkness. Out of the negative.
Up a level. Where the Hope dwells. One step at a time.

Towards and into the Light. Towards and into the Open Place.
Choosing to be led and formed by the Holy Spirit each day; filled and aware of the Grace and Healing provided daily in the Spirit of the Living God.

In Philippians 3:7-14, Paul writes of the decision we each come to, in the Discovery of the real value of finding the value of living our lives in the daily Encounter of the Open Place of our Creator's Presence.

Nothing can be compared to It. Nothing can be substituted for it.

"But all these things that I once thought very worthwhile–now I've thrown them all away so that I can put my trust and hope in Christ alone. Yes, everything else is worthless when compared with the priceless gain of knowing Christ Jesus my Lord. I have put aside all else, counting it worth less than nothing, in order that I can have Christ, and become one with him, no longer counting on being saved by being good enough or by obeying God's laws, but by trusting Christ to save me; for God's way of making us right with himself depends on faith–counting on Christ alone. Now I have given up everything else–I have found it to be the only way to really know Christ and to experience the mighty power that brought him back to life again, and to find out what it means to suffer and to die with him. So whatever it takes, I will be one who lives in the fresh newness of life of those who are alive from the dead.

"I don't mean to say I am perfect. I haven't learned all I should even yet, but I keep working toward that day when I will finally be all that Christ saved me for and wants me to be.

'No, dear brothers, I am still not all I should be, but I am bringing all my energies to bear on this one thing: Forgetting the past and **looking forward to what lies ahead**, I strain to reach the end of the race and receive the prize for which God is calling us up to heaven because of what Christ Jesus did for us."
(Philippians 3:7-14)

Considering the devotional text, please read the following verses, and make a few notes here of what discoveries occur to you regarding our Creator's view of people who make mistakes and/or bad decisions?

I John 1:8-9____

____

Psalm 37:23-24____

____

Psalm 145:14____

The Whole Heart Journey ™
Understanding the Process

Session Six –
"The Spirit of Adoption"

(Please begin watching the Video session for Session Six here. Write your notes below)

Luke 16:19-31

What are the Elements of the Light?

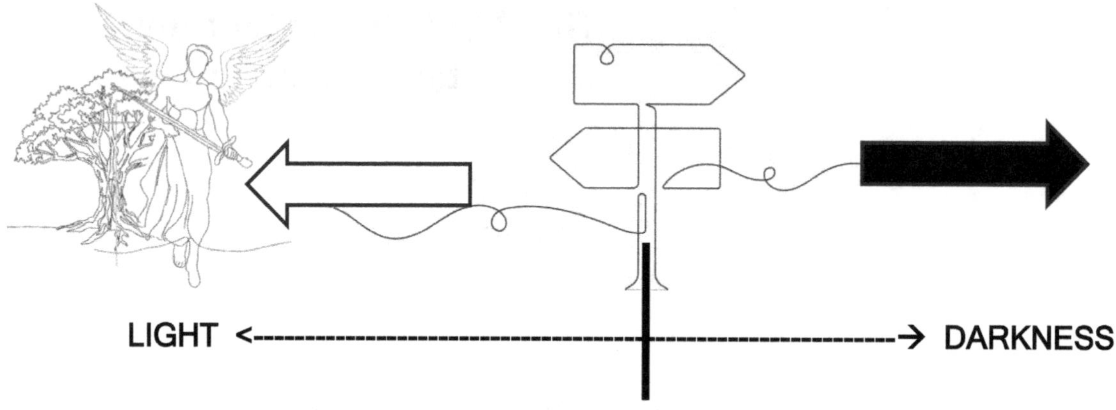

What are the Elements of the Darkness?

The Bruises of Satan

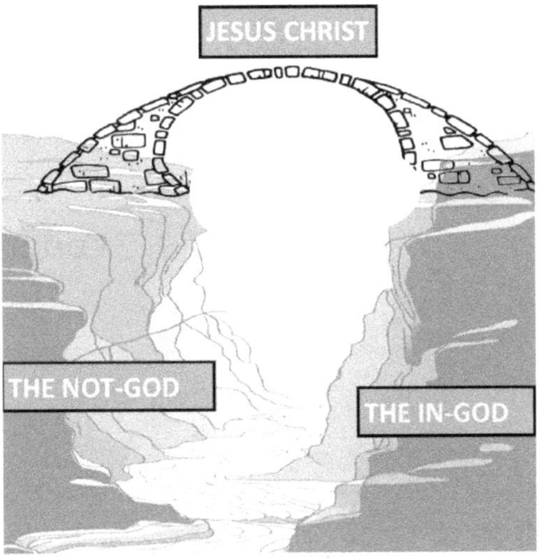

Colossians 1:19-20

I Timothy 2:5-6

So How Does "Being Adopted into the Kingdom" Work Exactly?

I Corinthians 13:12

James 1:22-25

II Corinthians 3:17-18

"meta-nay-oh"---

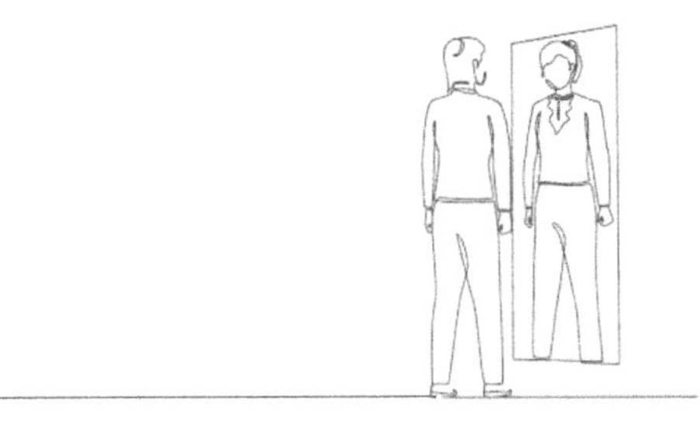

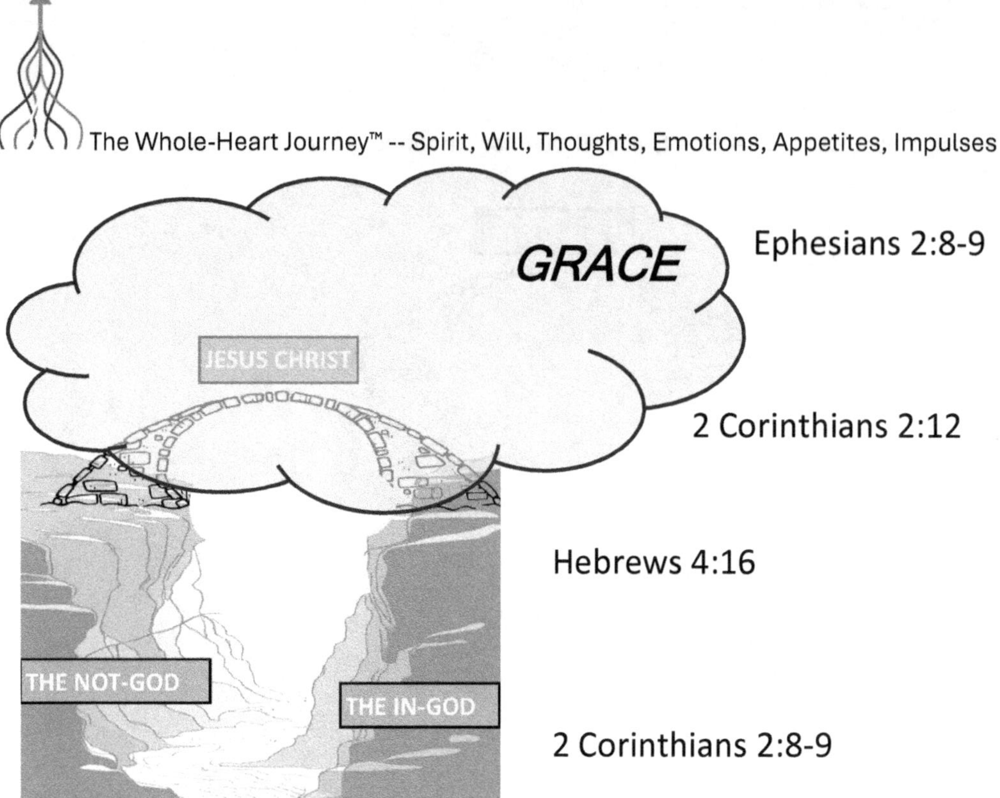

Ephesians 2:8-9

2 Corinthians 2:12

Hebrews 4:16

2 Corinthians 2:8-9

(Please work through the following Scriptures as the Video continues - with the music, doing the written work.)

1. What reason does Philippians 2:12-13 provide to help us understand why we are given the opportunities to make healthy choices?

____

____

2. What does Jude 1:24-25 teach us about one of the ministries of the Holy Spirit in our lives as Jesus-followers?

____

____

3. How does Psalm 40:2 describe the redemption experience when we are followers of our God?

____

(Please continue watching the video session here. Write your notes below)

The Spirit of Adoption

Romans 5:6-8

Romans 8:14-17

Growing and Developing in Jesus

Ephesians 4:13-15

(Please work through the Scripture study of John 5 below. Write your answers as the music continues.)

4. What does John 5:22 tell us about Father God's viewpoint of those Who choose to follow Jesus, and believe He is God come in human form?

---

5. Read the next verse: John 5:23. What does this verse tell us about how God the Father receives us, when we are born again?

---

6. In thinking about Jesus Christ being the Bridge between the "Not-God" and the "In-God," what does John 5:24 teach us about our position in God's eyes towards us?

---

7. What does this verse teach us about having been born again? Have we responded to the voice of God? Are we learning to recognize the voice of our Shepherd?

(Please continue watching the video session here. Write your notes below)

We live on the Bridge

I John 3:20-21

Romans 8:1

Please join us for the next step –

The Whole Heart Journey Program--
The Determinate Level

Session One – "Choosing My Focus"

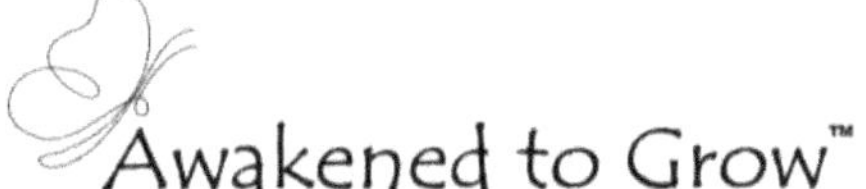

WholeHeartJourney.net

You can find the next class, in the Whole Heart Journey Class Series on wholeheartjourney.net . The Whole Heart Journey is a set of registered learning materials, for personal learning and growth in a Holy Spirit formed and led lifestyle.

The Whole Heart Journey consists of five segments. You have just completed the **Initiate Level, "Understanding the Process."** This level helps you to discover a healthy image of Creator God, our Abba Father.

The next class is the **Determinate Level, "Choosing My Focus."** This level will provide you with tools for building a healthy spiritual and emotional connection with God: The Father, the Son, and the Holy Spirit, through a step-by-step healing journey of the human will, mind, and emotions; your soul. You can find this class and its resources (videos and workbook) at **awakenedtogrow.com** On the **ATGstudies page. Or,** find us at **WholeHeartJourney.net.**

For more resources, encouragement and EQ tools, check out the collection of collaborative offerings from Awakened to Grow online.

AwakenedtoGrow.com *(Counseling and Coaching)*
AwakenedTeasandOils.com
AwakenedtoWorship.com
ATG Books.org
ATGStudies.com
NewVintageDesignCompany.com
TheCallInternational.com *(missions outreach)*

We are a charitable, nonprofit organization under the 501(c)3 of the Internal Revenue Code of the United States. A portion of every class/session/material requested fee is reinvested into our mission to serve those who cannot afford to pursue help.

www.ingramcontent.com/pod-product-compliance
Lightning Source LLC
LaVergne TN
LVHW081414110826
845149LV00010B/1736

9780989321495